CHILDREN
APRONS

# FAMILY LONDON

## FUN DAYS OUT WITH CHILDREN FROM TOTS TO TEENS

### JIMI FAMUREWA

#### PHOTOGRAPHS BY CAMILLE MACK

FRANCES
LINCOLN

# CONTENTS

# INTRODUCTION

Escaping the rain in a soft play dungeon while others hit the pub;
traipsing to the same playground as a city festival echoes in
the distance; shelling out for chicken nuggets as friends visit
some buzzy new brunch spot – yes, being a parent can occasionally
make you feel like you're on the fringes of all things exciting
happening in the capital. Thankfully, it doesn't have to be this
way. In recent years, London's wider cultural renaissance (the
resurgent culinary scene, its world-renowned museums, the areas
jolted to life by the 2012 Olympics) has spilled over into an
array of attractions that loudly proclaim their family-friendly
credentials. But which ones are actually worth visiting? That's
where this book comes in. From under-the-radar gems and bucket
list big hitters to kid-ready cafés and spectacular outdoor
spaces, within these pages you'll find an exhaustively researched
edit of the unforgettable London experiences capable of keeping
all ages happy. So break the monotony and dive in – there's a
family-sized adventure here for everyone.

# PARKS, PLAYGROUNDS & SECRET GARDENS

# PARKS, PLAYGROUNDS & SECRET GARDENS

Whether you're pushing swings, pelting after a scooter-riding thrill seeker or kicking a football, parenthood all but guarantees that you'll spend a lot of time in parks. And, with 47 per cent of the capital given over to open space, there's a leafy spot to suit every mood. Of course, it would be a fool's errand to try to list every passable patch of grass in London, but in this section you'll find unexpected one-offs, ranging from a glimmering indoor garden 160 metres above the city to a man-made mountain range that's perfect for mini adventurers. There's also kiddie-friendly coordinates to save you a long traipse around big-hitters like Hampstead Heath and Victoria Park. Here's where to vote green.

## CORAM'S FIELDS

There was a time when this Bloomsbury park and playground – unexpectedly positioned smack bang in the centre of London – was a hushed secret among in-the-know parents. Survey the queue of kids waiting for a turn on its popular zip-line in the school holidays and you will sensibly assume that word has got out. But Coram's Fields (London's first public children's playground, on the site of a former eighteenth-century home for unwanted babies) is still very much one to have in your parental arsenal for any West End excursions. (You may also be happy to hear of their after-school playscheme.) A giant sandpit, paddling pool, sprawling play space, small city farm and café are among the myriad delights. And, for extra peace of mind, no adult can enter the park without a child.

—

93 Guilford Street, WC1N 1DN.
020 7837 6138
www.coramsfields.org
Russell Square tube.

## CRYSTAL PALACE PARK

With its transmitter tower, destroyed glass monolith and secret Victorian subway, this South London spot has the sort of rich history that some municipal spaces would kill for. But if you're taking junior guests here, the sculptures of prehistoric creatures are the undeniable stars of the show. Originally revealed in 1854 (and given a much needed refurb in 2002) these looming figures were the first dinosaur recreations in the world and, although they're now notorious for their misshapen inaccuracies, kids will get a guaranteed kick out of finding them lurking next to the evocative lake. There are real animals on offer at the nearby city farm and the brutalist sports centre in the middle of the park hosts remote controlled car races at weekends.

—

Ledrington Road, SE19 2GA.
0300 303 8658
www.cpdinosaurs.org
Crystal Palace rail and Overground.

## CAMLEY STREET NATURAL PARK

A short stumble from the screaming mayhem of Granary Square's spurting fountains, this compact but utterly captivating nature reserve is one of those 'I can't believe this is here!' surprises that has the power to floor even lifelong Londoners. Set behind King's Cross station on the site of a former coal yard, Camley Street fringes the Regents Canal and encompasses floating walkways (the pyramid-like Viewpoint pontoon, designed by The Finnish Institute, is a particular favourite with young explorers) and pleasingly overgrown paths across two acres of peaceful greenery. There's wildlife to spot (including kingfishers, geese, and mini-beasts in a signposted dipping pond), and from spring to autumn the Wildwood Café is the perfect stop off for tea, coffee or punchy veggie food.

---

12 Camley Street, N1C 4PW.
020 7833 2311
www.kingscross.co.uk/camley-street-natural-park
King's Cross St Pancras rail and tube.

## VICTORIA PARK

Boating lake, Chinese pagoda, annual winter festival: this all-singing, all-dancing East End site (the first London park specifically constructed for public use) has pretty much everything. That said, shrewd parents will want to make a pilgrimage to the east side to sample the Pools Playground area. Dominated by a set of formidably huge slides and bordered by other clever time-killers (rope nests, skate park, musical slabs for stomping out a tune), it's also within scrambling distance of a water area – switched on in late spring – which takes the form of an undulating urban beach. The Park Café, which serves an Indian-themed menu complete with addictive samosas, is nearby, but the lakeside Pavilion bakery and café is a local hit worth the slight hike.

—

Grove Road, E3 5TB.
020 8985 5699
www.towerhamlets.gov.uk
Bethnal Green tube.

## KEW GARDENS

With fantastic free parks littering the capital, a green space needs to be special to justify charging an entry fee. Kew – blessed with botanical gardens, a teetering Chinese Pagoda and much, much more – delivers in spades, and offers value with free entry for under-4s and an appealing membership offer. It's a dauntingly huge 300-acre site, but youngsters should be coaxed to the Climbers and Creepers indoor play area and the treetop walkway (be warned that prams have to be left on the forest floor). Then there's the Hive – a relatively recent addition that uses a buzzing, flickering 17-metre-high installation set amid wildflowers to explore the importance of British bees. Not even the regular rumble of Heathrow-bound aeroplanes can spoil a day here.

—

Kew Road, TW9 3AB.

020 8332 5655

www.kew.org

Kew Gardens tube and Overground.

## DIANA, PRINCESS OF WALES PLAYGROUND

Built in the shadow of her Kensington Palace apartments, this child-friendly tribute to the late Princess of Wales is worthy of its reputation as the grand-daddy of London playgrounds. Brave the occasional queue at the gate and a commendably detailed and beautifully designed dreamworld awaits. There's a fitting Neverland theme to the under-12s enclosure (author J. M. Barrie used Kensington Gardens as a constant setting for his Peter Pan tales), and a beached pirate ship is the ever-mobbed centrepiece to hidden areas encompassing teepees, a treehouse, a sea monster, water play, a sunken treasure chest and untold other sensory delights. It's inclusively designed for children with special needs and inaccessible to unaccompanied adults.

—

Broad Walk, W2 2UH.
0300 061 2001
www.royalparks.org.uk
Queensway tube.

## HOBBLEDOWN

Tucked just inside the M25, this Epsom attraction probably shares more DNA with nearby theme park Chessington World of Adventures than your average local stretch of grass. As well as mazes, intricate scrambling tunnels, exotic animals, giant bouncing pillows and more outdoors, a modest entry fee unlocks all manner of indoor delights, all laser-targeted at a young audience. The aggressive medieval theming (Hobbledown is peopled by fictional singing characters called the Hobblers and heavily influenced by the fairy tale-styling of the huge adventure parks dotted all over Germany) may set some parental teeth on edge. But under-10s will lap it up and the exhilarating high rope challenges and zip line should satisfy buccaneering big kids.

—

Horton Lane, Epsom, Surrey, KT19 8PT.
0843 289 4979
www.hobbledown.com
Epsom rail.

## HAMPSTEAD HEATH

It may act as a kind of overgrown back garden for some of North London's flashiest residents, but Hampstead Heath still has the power to feel like a truly peaceful and untrammelled hideaway. Bikeable or hikeable family options abound: a grand lunch at the Kenwood House café, massive playing fields, a toddler-sized hollow tree near the Mixed Bathing Pond, and the windblown lookout of Kite Hill (or Parliament Hill), which is particularly worth dragging your rabble to. The view from here certainly deserves its status as one of the finest in the capital. Plus, on snowy days, it's a high-quality sledding spot, and in warmer months the brightly-coloured playground and lido – lined with stainless steel like a giant shimmering sink – welcome crowds of grateful families.

—

East Heath Road, NW3 1TH.
020 7332 3322
www.cityoflondon.gov.uk
Hampstead Heath rail and Overground.

## BROCKWELL PARK

There's more to this Herne Hill expanse of green than its popular – if bracingly cold – 1930s lido. On sunny days, runners, IPA-sipping Brixtonites, dog-walkers and sprinting kids all coexist across more than 125 acres of diverse space (including a paddling pool, duck pond, nineteenth-century hall-cum-tea room and excellent community greenhouse), and that mix of visitors stops it all feeling like a giant playground. Not that there aren't plenty of distractions for little ones.

On Sundays between April and October a miniature railway offers short rides that are always a hit with preschoolers, and the Lambeth Country Fair – a giddy jamboree of live reggae, farm animals, vegetable sculptures and industrial-strength local cider – is an absolute must in the summer.

—

Norwood Road, SE24 9BJ.
020 7274 3088 (Brockwell Lido)
www.brockwellpark.com
Herne Hill rail.

## ALEXANDRA PARK

If you're looking for the best pedalos in London, shaped like dragons, VW Beetles and the classic giant swans, then the lake outside Ally Pally is where to hit the water. Eye-catching boats are only a small slice of the afternoon-soaking attractions within the grounds of this illustrious Victorian events space, sport venue and onetime base for the BBC. There's pitch and putt golf, tree-climbing, a somewhat gnarly skatepark and a couple of reliable indoor options should rain clouds spoil that terrific view. Younger kids will enjoy clattering around the Little Dinosaurs soft play and older members of your brood can practice their off-season pirouettes at one of London's few year-round indoor ice rinks.

—

Alexandra Palace Way, N22 7AY.
020 8365 212
www.alexandrapalace.com
Alexandra Palace rail.

## SKY GARDEN

Dubbed the Walkie Talkie (and, for a period, the 'Walkie Scorchie' thanks to a since-rectified habit of heating the streets below on sunny days), 20 Fenchurch Street has recovered from its difficult birth to earn its place on the London skyline. How? With its innovative, vertiginous public oasis. Free to enter (although tickets must be booked in advance online) and surprisingly child friendly (expect to see little tykes pushing the squishy log-shaped seats around), it's a truly transcendent space with banked planters of eucalyptus, sage, towering palm trees and more sheltering hidden benches, a restaurant, a café and unmatched panoramas of the ever-changing cityscape – just as impressive in the evenings as on a clear summer's day. Food and drink prices are suitably sky high, but there are few better places to spend an awestruck afternoon.

—

Philpot Lane, EC3M 8AF.

0333 772 0020

skygarden.london

Monument or Cannon Street tube.

## NORTHALA FIELDS

It may look like a UFO landing site but this quartet of grassy mounds a short shuffle from Northolt station may well point to the sustainable future of man-made park spaces. Opened in 2008, these eye-catching hillocks are made from the piled rubble excavated for nearby construction projects – including the demolition of the old Wembley Stadium and the building of Westfield – and saved 60,000 lorryloads of spoil heading to landfill. So it's green in more ways than one. Not that kids will be too fussed about all that as they dash up a spiral pathway to the summit, gaze out at the jumble of distant London landmarks, join the weekend kite fliers or scamper to the log-lined playground below.

—

Kensington Road, Northalt, UB5 6UR.
020 8825 5000
www.ealing.gov.uk
Northolt tube.

## THE LINE

Launched in 2015, this free sculpture trail linking the O2 in Greenwich and Stratford's Olympic Park may not seem the most obvious option for parents. But the fact that it requires a trip on the Emirates Air Line cable car – a dangling white elephant reborn as one of the capital's most enjoyable forms of family transportation – makes it essential. After a stunning ten-minute ride (or 'flight', to use their slightly heavy-handed parlance), you land in the Royal Docks and make your way past striking works like Damien Hirst's magnified skin fleck, Sterling Ruby's abstract cannon – which few kids can resist climbing on – and a giant twirl of trolleys by Abigail Fallis. An enlightening, alternative park in a too often forgotten corner of the capital.

—

Edmund Halley Way, SE10 0FR.
No phone.
www.the-line.org
North Greenwich tube.

## DULWICH PARK

Ambling distance from the pocket of semi-rural calm that is Dulwich Village, this looker of a South-East London space is relatively young in park terms (it was hewn from farmland and opened in 1890). It finds room for all the usual crowd-pleasers – a buggy-packed café, busy playground, boating lake and sports pitches – but the real appeal here is its doughnut-like shape. The wide, traffic-free orbital path is a hit with local runners, as well as recumbent bikes (low-slung, pedal-powered hire trikes of varying sizes), which can regularly be seen whipping around the leafy circuit. They are a great way to amuse older children likely to roll their eyes at another set of swings and a climbing frame.

—

College Road, SE21 7BQ.
020 7525 2000
www.southwark.gov.uk
West Dulwich rail.

### RUISLIP LIDO

Asked to name a beach in the capital, most Londoners would probably go for one of the muddy banks lapped by the unappetisingly murky waters of the Thames. This West London expanse of imported sand by a freshwater lake is a more preferable answer. Surrounded by a dense forest and peppered with all manner of other sunny day treats (playground, decent gastropub, splash park), it's also worth visiting for a ride on the Ruislip Lido Railway: a regular, volunteer-run service of miniature diesel and locomotive trains that is so popular with families it's normal to find an open-top carriage crammed with buggies on a sunny Saturday. A warning: the shallow water and grimy silt underfoot make proper swimming a tricky prospect.

—

Reservoir Road, HA4 7TY.
01895 250 111
www.hillingdon.gov.uk
Ruislip tube.

## FIVE MORE:

- **Coldfall Wood**
  Fallen branches, creaking wooden walkways and a dense thicket of trees beckon at this gorgeous ancient site in Muswell Hill. A great nature trail and packed family events schedule help things along.
  *Creighton Avenue, N10 1NT.*
  *www.coldfallwoods.co.uk*

- **Thames Barrier Park**
  An undervisited marvel in the shadow of London's glistening flood-prevention fins. Sunken gardens, a lovely café, rollercoaster topiary and green hills just begging to be rolled down.
  *North Woolwich Road, E16 2HP.*
  *www.royalgreenwich.gov.uk*

- **Holland Park**
  Avoid the the roaring supercars of Kensington in this haven of tumbling waterfalls and Japanese plant life. Hit the den-building area and keep an eye out for peacocks.
  *Ilchester Place, W8 6LU.*
  *www.rbkc.gov.uk*

- **Dalston Eastern Curve Garden**
  A rugged community sanctuary and café in the hipsterville bullseye with a fleet of careworn vehicles for the kids, potent filter coffee for the grown-ups and exceptional homemade cakes for everyone.
  *13 Dalston Lane, E8 3DF.*
  *www.dalstongarden.org*

- **Ladywell Fields**
  An ever-tranquil interconnected collection of green South-East London walkways. Playgrounds, a community café, iron pumps for water play and a trickling stream perfect for a quick paddle.
  *Ladywell Road, SE13 7UT.*
  *www.lewisham.gov.uk*

# MUSEUMS & GALLERIES

# MUSEUMS & GALLERIES

As anyone who has been patted down for entry into some
provincial hall of dusty glass cabinets will attest,
London truly leads the way when it comes to museums and
galleries. There are more than 200 of them within the M25 and,
crucially, they are often cheap or completely free. What's
more, a combination of shelter, scampering space and hands-on
attractions aimed at enquiring young minds ensure these places
are a constant sanctuary for families. Yes, it's hard to avoid
the allure (or the crowds) of the Victorian-built behemoths
on Kensington's Exhibition Road, but hidden corners offer
surprising pleasures. From modern art and exotic taxidermy
to mini vehicles and eye-popping artefacts, here's where
to pair killing time with cultural nourishment.

## HORNIMAN MUSEUM AND GARDENS

Perhaps best-known for the overstuffed walrus that stands proud in the main hall, this South-East London palace of anthropology, natural history and more is a veritable fantasia for families. In fact, with its sprawling gardens, 1,300 musical instruments, taxidermy, working beehive, adjacent farm and basement aquarium, the term 'museum' does it a disservice. The Horniman may be relatively small but it packs a breathless amount in – there's even a handling collection of masks and curios that fly in the face of the usual 'do not touch' signs – and it knows its young, energetic audience incredibly well. The busy café isn't bad either. Embrace the bedlam and expect a few pleading requests for a return trip.

—

100 London Road, SE23 3PQ.
020 8699 1872
www.horniman.ac.uk
Forest Hill rail and Overground.

## LONDON TRANSPORT MUSEUM

The train of buggies stretching back towards the entrance should be your first clue that children are very fond of this blockbusting Covent Garden museum. School parties in hi-vis vests weave between the vintage buses downstairs during term time, and the All Aboard play zone – with its costumes, Thames Nipper boat and 'drivable' bus – can occasionally feel a touch too close to the real claustrophobia of rush hour public transport. There's always somewhere to escape to though. And the sheer breadth of cleverly conceived options here (vintage posters, tube-driving simulations, pre-war upper floor exhibits to keep the slightly older set stimulated) help it appeal to more than just tiny train enthusiasts.

—

Covent Garden Piazza, WC2E 7BB.
020 7379 6344
www.ltmuseum.co.uk
Covent Garden tube.

## NATIONAL MARITIME MUSEUM

The Cutty Sark, with its chequered history (it was damaged by fire in 2007 and 2014) and prime Thameside location, is a reliable tractor beam for tourist families ambling through Greenwich. But if you're really in the know? Well, you go to this free, terrifically designed celebration of Britain's seafaring history on the edge of the pretty royal park. The AHOY! gallery – a play space with docker-themed stacking blocks, a pretend fish market and myriad other miniature delights – is unbeatable for preschoolers. There's also an older top-floor exhibit that gives kids a gruesome rat-filled guide to life below deck and the interactive Great Map floor has a café that acts as a useful holding pen for knackered parents.

—

Romney Road, SE10 9NF.
020 8312 6608
www.rmg.co.uk
Greenwich rail or Cutty Sark for Maritime Greenwich DLR.

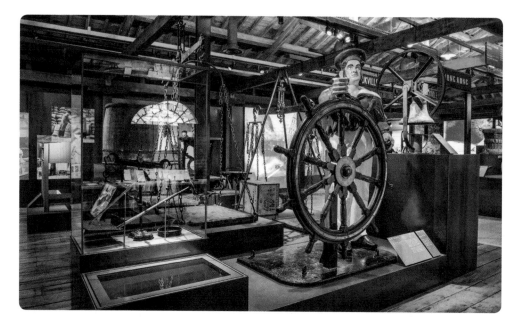

## MUSEUM OF LONDON

The murky facts of this city's journey, from a group of prehistoric villages and subsequent Roman capital to our current bustling metropolis, are characterfully brought to life at these twinned, Museum of London locations. The City branch at London Wall is thoughtfully interactive and mixes the new (you're met by a digital panorama of 24 hours in London) and the old (an eighteenth-century jail cell) with vivid panache. The Docklands outpost is also worth a visit. Those not spooked by the dark will enjoy stalking the authentically grubby streets that make up the Sailortown Gallery, as well as Mudlarks – an exhibit for under-8s with giant building blocks, model docks, padded areas and an excellent shore-themed water table. It's a terrific play area served with a side order of historical context.

—

150 London Wall, EC2Y 5HN.
020 7001 9844
www.museumoflondon.org.uk
Barbican or St Paul's tube.
**BRANCHES:** Docklands E14 4AL.

## SCIENCE MUSEUM

Nestled next door to the Natural History Museum (see page 46), this dauntingly good house of learning might have the edge over its dino-stuffed neighbour when it comes to pre-school visitors. The jewel in its crown is the downstairs Garden area that introduces three- to six-year-old guests in adorable aprons to the world of science with splash-happy water play, light games and pipes that carry sound. Bigger kids have been known to be equally enraptured. From a fragment of lunar rock and the world's oldest locomotive to Wonderlab (the recently rebooted interactive gallery that now, contentiously, carries a small entry fee), it's a mind-expanding day out.

---

Exhibition Road, SW7 2DD.
020 7942 4000
www.sciencemuseum.org.uk
South Kensington tube.

## NATURAL HISTORY MUSEUM

Setting off at dawn, going in with a meticulous plan, visiting on a weekday – parents tend to approach an encounter with this wildly popular institution like a particularly gruelling extreme sport. And with more than five million visitors a year, its colour-coded zones can be an overwhelmingly busy place. But if you abandon hope of beating the crush and sharpen your elbows, its seemingly endless attractions – ranging from guaranteed eye-poppers like the life-size blue whale to the twisted casts of Pompeii residents – are well worth it. Be aware that the atmospheric noises in the Red Zone may be too much for some junior explorers and don't ignore the pricey but special Dino Snores sleepovers for seven- to eleven-year-olds.

—

Cromwell Road, SW7 5BD.
020 7942 5725
www.nhm.ac.uk
South Kensington tube.

## V&A MUSEUM OF CHILDHOOD

A museum with various enticing antique toys behind glass cases may sound like a peculiar kind of torture for most kids, but there's plenty to cushion the blow here. Dominated by a bustling central café and an overbrimming gift shop, this grand former repository for leftovers from the Grand Exhibition makes room for two floors of informative hands-on attractions and play spaces. These range from a beach-themed indoor sandpit and building block area to an old-fashioned shrunken kitchen and a pair of ever-popular rocking horses. Smaller gurglers are catered for with a compact sensory area and the temporary exhibitions (often themed around popular children's authors or classic characters) are always popular.

—

Cambridge Heath Road, E2 9PA.
020 8983 5200
www.vam.ac.uk/moc
Bethnal Green tube.

## RAF MUSEUM LONDON

Located near the upper tip of the Northern Line, this high-flying attraction probably isn't on the radar of as many families as it should be. Very good news if you don't like the scrums that come with most decent museums. Free to enter, it's old-fashioned in the best sense (there's a large indoor picnic area and the Blitz-themed café does a fantastic 'Ripping' Plum Cake based on one that decorated First World War pilot Albert Ball used to keep in his cockpit). Its cavernous hangars contain more than 100 different aircrafts and a pulse-pounding 4D theatre. Yes, Aeronauts – the interactive kids area – may be slightly worn-in, but its helicopters, miniature planes and whirring bits of aeronautical ephemera have real, addictive charm.

—

Grahame Park Way, NW9 5LL.
020 8205 2266
www.rafmuseum.org.uk
Colindale tube.

## TATE MODERN

The brutalist concrete interior of the Tate's outpost on the South Bank holds many carefully considered and appealing family facilities (abundant café options, a free cloakroom for scooters, the climb-able benches that fringe the Turbine Hall's main ramp). It's really an underrated treasure. The jagged 2016 extension that is the Switch House has striking interactive sculptures and one of London's best top-floor panoramas, the Start Display's vibrant pieces are always a hit and the digital doodling screens at the Drawing Bar offer a great time-soak. Most enticingly, this is an inspiring all-weather space that subtly combines kid-friendly visual stimulation with something grown-ups can chew over.

—

Bankside, SE1 9TG.
020 7887 8888
www.tate.org.uk
Blackfriars or Southwark tube.

## THE CARTOON MUSEUM

Not far from the forest of selfie sticks outside the British Museum, this characterful micro-gallery offers something infinitely more peaceful. Upstairs, there are eye-catching giant character cut-outs, drawing materials and a huge stack of comics (a must for Beano and Dandy aficionados) that are perfect for impulsive trips. Alternatively, aim to co-ordinate your visit with one of the events or summer workshops – especially as they have a pesky habit of selling out. Your budding cartoonists can try everything from claymation and Manga drawing to digital comic book making and superhero caricatures. They'll even lay on tea and biscuits for a small fee if you ring ahead – as sure a sign as any that this is a little gem, run with love and infectious enthusiasm.

—

35 Little Russell Street, WC1A 2HH.
020 7580 8155
www.cartoonmuseum.org
Holborn or Tottenham Court Road tube.

# GRAND DAYS OUT

# GRAND DAYS OUT

Most London parents have a complex relationship with blockbuster
attractions. Yes, these birthday treats or end-of-the-holiday
blowouts are meant to be facilitators of unbridled familial joy.
But the mere thought of them – the crowds, the high stakes, the
wallet-emptying expense – can bring some out in a cold sweat.
Rather than fretting, it's far better to choose wisely, do
your research and just embrace the mayhem of places that will
undoubtedly bring you into the orbit of the capital's
18.6 million annual visitors. Here then, covering everything
from an avant-garde helter skelter to a close encounter with
an Asiatic lion, is a guide to the best of these slickly run
big beasts – and how to escape them with your sanity intact.

## QUEEN ELIZABETH OLYMPIC PARK

Not all top-tier family days out come with a whacking payment receipt. Most of the diverse diversions at London's newest green space – the wide bike-friendly pathways, treehouse-filled Tumbling Bay Playground, squirting water jets, two-tiered red climbing wall – are absolutely free, but there's a week's worth of options if you do want to spend some cash. Swimming obsessives can enter the curved bulk of the London Aquatics Centre (the inflatable-hopping Aqua Splash

sessions are heaps of fun), budding BMXers can hit the Velo Park, and then there's ArcelorMittal Orbit. Anish Kapoor's mangled tower divided opinion in 2012, but it's since been fitted with a hit 15mph tunnel slide that lets hardy over-8s take the express route to the bottom.

—

Olympic Park Avenue, E20 2ST.
0800 072 2110
www.queenelizabetholympicpark.co.uk
Stratford rail, tube, DLR and Overground.

58

## ◀ SEA LIFE LONDON AQUARIUM

Nestled on the same stretch of the South Bank as The London Eye and The London Dungeon, this big-hitter is as famous for its crowds and prices as its sea creatures. The occasional pedestrian gridlock – not helped by the fact that you follow a set route – isn't so bad once you're in it, and older wannabe marine biologists in particular (not likely to be spooked by the darkened warren of tanks) will find plenty of distraction. There's an atmospherically chilly penguin area, a Shark Walk that will draw gasps, a cavernous manta ray area (with added dinosaur bones) and, of course, a crowd-pleasing chance to spot Nemo-like clown fish. A watery labyrinth that, especially in off-peak hours, just about justifies the hefty outlay.

—

County Hall, Westminster Bridge Road, SE1 7PB.
0871 663 1678
www2.visitsealife.com/london
Waterloo or Westminster tube.

## MADAME TUSSAUDS

Few things perplex cynical Londoners like the early morning queues that form outside the original Madame Tussauds. The truth is, more than 130 years after it opened, this tourist-facing Marylebone beacon really does offer families more than just dusty celebrity waxworks. As well as impressively topical selfie-fodder (300 figures of everyone from the Royal Family and Rihanna to Benedict Cumberbatch and Usain Bolt), there are cleverly conceived immersive experiences that score highly with kids. The juddering taxi tour of London's history is a hoot, the shriek-prompting Chamber of Horrors plays well with older children and the show-stopping Star Wars exhibit will thrill any young Padawans.

—

Marylebone Road, NW1 5LR.
0871 894 3000
www.madametussauds.co.uk
Baker Street tube.

## HAMPTON COURT PALACE

London is not lacking in lavish historic residences (Eltham Palace, for example, is a favourite of shrewd South London parents), but how many of them have a smoke-belching dragon out back? This 25-foot-long mystical creature – normally being clambered on by giddy children – is the centrepiece of The Magic Garden, a recent addition that opens from spring to mid-autumn each year and also features splash-happy stepping stones, slides, a sandpit and structures based on the Tiltyard Towers erected for Tudor tournaments. You can pay for entry to just this area and the enjoyably bewildering maze, or top up to enter the palace itself and explore Henry VIII's gilded playpen (made easy by the family trail maps available from the Information Centre).

—

Hampton Court Road, Surrey, KT8 9AU.
020 3166 6000
www.hrp.org.uk/hampton-court-palace
Hampton Court rail.

## LONDON ZOO ZSL

As the world's oldest scientific zoo and host to more than 1.2 million visitors a year, the sprawling animal kingdom at Regent's Park could easily rest on its laurels. However, from the moment you follow the parade of families through the entrance (note that booking online lets you jump the queue) the most striking thing about the London Zoological Society's flagship facility is its constant commitment to innovation, conservation and shiny new features. From the Indian-themed Land of the Lions and walkthrough lemur exhibit to the nerve-jangling spider enclosure and sub-aquatic Penguin Beach observation dome, every corner packs an intelligently curated, informative surprise. It's expensive and energy-sapping but totally, utterly brilliant.

—

Regent's Park, NW1 4RY.
020 7722 3333
www.zsl.org
Camden Town tube.

## BUCKINGHAM PALACE

Not many kids will be able to resist a nose around the Queen's digs and – while the Royal Family are off on their summer holidays – the State Rooms at Buckingham Palace are opened to the public. It may sound odd, given the rabble of smartphone-wielding tourists outside, but it's one of the capital's most underrated family days out – the sort of thing sniffy native Londoners will dismiss as just for visitors. More fool them. A regally-priced ticket (happily halved for under-17s, while under-5s go free) gets you a slick tour of the grand gardens and history-steeped interiors (spotting the Queen's secret door to her apartment will keep any grumblers occupied) and a designated kids area piled with books, costumes and hats combats any perceived fustiness.

—

Buckingham Palace, SW1A 1AA.
0303 123 7300
www.royalcollection.org.uk
St James's Park tube.

## LEGOLAND WINDSOR RESORT

Pitched at the pre-teen audience too young for the stomach-lurching thrills of nearby Thorpe Park, this bricktastic Berkshire attraction teems with so many precision-engineered pleasures you'd be forgiven for thinking it had been designed by kids. The Duplo-themed splash park, a dragon-shaped rollercoaster, Miniland's shrunken London skyline, the piratical play area, wildly popular electric driving school and countless other innovations (all constructed from more than 80 million Lego bricks) will leave parents scrambling to keep up. Naturally, this also translates to big crowds – even arriving early during school holidays only brings slender rewards – so it may be wise to splash out even more on a Q-Bot: the pricey but sanity-saving queue-jumping gizmo.

—

Winfield Road, Windsor, Berkshire, SL4 4AY.
0871 222 2001
www.legoland.co.uk
Windsor & Eton Central or Riverside rail.

## WARNER BROS. STUDIO TOUR LONDON – THE MAKING OF HARRY POTTER

The ever-crowded but dinky Platform 9¾ exhibit in King's Cross station will only sate a Hogwarts obsessive for so long. For a real hit of Pottermania your best bet is this spot just outside Watford: the production hub for the Harry Potter films that has been cannily turned into a vault of memorabilia, immaculate sets and movie-making insight. Tickets are set to allotted time slots and are not cheap (£35 for an adult and a whopping £27 for over-5s), but it's an expertly curated day out brimming with magic touches that will send muggles into raptures. Wander into the Great Hall at Hogwarts, stroll down the magical Diagon Alley and slurp a syrupy cup of butterbeer. Warning: you will be begged for a gift shop wand.

—

Studio Tour Drive, Leavesden, WD25 7LR.
0345 084 0900
www.wbstudiotour.co.uk
Watford Junction rail.

# WHERE THE WILD THINGS ARE

# WHERE THE WILD THINGS ARE

London may be an ever-expanding tangle of concrete and gleaming glass but it also harbours wildlife that goes beyond pigeons, park ducks and increasingly brazen gangs of foxes. From roaming deer and leaping lemurs to wallabies and alpacas, there are surprising creatures in every corner of the capital. Yes, a diverse array of city farms — originated by the band of early 1970s pioneers who turned a disused Kentish Town timberyard into London's first rural hideaway — are dotted all over the capital. But they're only half the story when it comes to discovering the city's wild side. Here's where to thrill your kids by bringing them face to face (or snout, or beak) with animals they've possibly only glimpsed in books.

## LONDON WETLAND CENTRE

Not all West Londoners will know that there's an enormous nature reserve right under their noses. You need only make the trip to this Barnes hideaway in the kink of the Thames near Hammersmith to get a taste for the wild within sight of the city's towering spires. Each corner of this 105-acre site brims with birds, insects and other unexpected wildlife. The three-story Peacock Tower hide offers occasional views of grazing highland cattle and ordinarily camera-shy otters are often willing to put on a playful show. What's more, there's a decent adventure playground, the requisite café (picnic tables for those who come prepared), a toddler-friendly Pond Zone and all manner of interesting sculptures waiting to be discovered. Entry is free for under-4s and events (including the raucous annual Puddle Jumping Championships) should be added to the calendar.

—

Queen Elizabeth's Walk, SW13 9WT.
020 8409 4400
www.wwt.org.uk
Barnes rail.

## HACKNEY CITY FARM

London, and particularly East London, has its fair share of good city farms for those families that love the smell of manure in the morning (Mudchute in the Docklands springs to mind). But stop by this place on the edge of Haggerston Park and you can see why it's so enduringly popular with hip local parents. There's a bustling courtyard area with lively roaming ducks and chickens, a beautiful allotment-style garden and a bigger pasture area home to sheep, donkeys, tree-nibbling goats and – this being London – opportunistic pigeons swiping food. Then there's the exceptional Frizzante café: a hideaway bestrewn with paper lanterns and mismatched furniture where they make their own ice cream and as much produce as possible comes direct from the farm.

—

1A Goldsmiths Row, E2 8QA.
020 7729 6381
www.hackneycityfarm.co.uk
Cambridge Heath rail and Overground.

## BATTERSEA PARK CHILDREN'S ZOO

While it's widely acknowledged that zoos mostly appeal to a junior clientele, kids officially rule the roost at this toddler-friendly, family-run attraction on the northern perimeter of Battersea Park. For starters, there aren't many serious zoological facilities where a real, rideable fire engine is one of the most popular attractions. Still, there's a nice range of animals if you can coax kids from the various play areas and a popular parked-up tractor. Farmyard regulars, wallabies and a range of high-flying monkeys are in attendance, and the meerkat area (complete with observation tunnel) is brilliantly designed. Entry can seem steep for very large groups, and be prepared: you enter and exit through the cuddly toy-stuffed gift shop.

—

Chelsea Bridge Gate, SW11 4NJ.
020 7924 5826
www.batterseaparkzoo.co.uk
Battersea Park rail and Overground.

## LEE VALLEY PARK FARMS

Technically two conjoined facilities in one, this Waltham Abbey monster boasts a lot more than the usual cow and chicken yards all over London. In fact, you may find yourself struggling to sell the prospect of viewing animals in the face of a lively soft play barn, outdoor area with irresistible giant jumping pillow, astroturfed toboggan run and mini pedal tractors. The critters are absolutely worth dragging them away for, though. Digging sand right next to scuttling meerkats is a surefire hit, watching racing pigs and sheep will get the blood-pumping, bearded dragons will impress the dinosaur-obsessed and a visit to the working dairy farm – via a bumpy trip in a giant tractor – is an informative eye-opener about just where all that cereal milk comes from.

----

Stubbins Hall Lane, Waltham Abbey, Essex, EN9 2EF.
01992 892 781
www.lvfarms.co.uk
Cheshunt rail and Overground.

## WOODLANDS FARM TRUST

Some city farms, for better or worse, feel like slick operations hemmed in by dual carriageways and railway lines. But this working 89-acre site a short drive from Greenwich gives the young and welly-booted a feel of life on a real working farm. Fringed by a thicket of trees and entered through a swing gate, it's a secret rural treasure that has pigs (including a Gloucestershire Old Spot called Rosie), sheep, cattle, roaming ducks and a dipping pond for mini-beast hunting excursions. Also, there's a carved wooden play tractor, a rustic café open at weekends and during school holidays (it's cash-only and there are perilously prominent ice cream signs), and the whole thing has an appealingly rough-edged feel.

—

331 Shooters Hill, Welling, Kent, DA16 3RP.
020 8319 8900
www.thewoodlandsfarmtrust.org
Falconwood or Welling rail.

## GOLDERS HILL PARK ZOO

One of only two free registered zoos in London (Hanwell Zoo is the other – see page 91), this small but lovingly run menagerie on the outer edge of Hampstead Heath boasts a surprisingly diverse range of animals. A short amble from the idyllic trickle of the park's water garden you'll find ring-tailed lemurs, badger-ish coatis, laughing kookaburras, a mini herd of red deer and others in spacious green enclosures. What's more there's a high quality café, the bronze Golders Hill Girl statue (a lounging figure young ones love to drape themselves over), and a compact, muggy butterfly house. Keep your eyes peeled for prehistoric creatures too: a trio of rusty dinosaur sculptures by Jake and Dinos Chapman lurk on one of the immaculate lawns.

—

West Heath Avenue, NW11 7QP.
020 7332 3511
www.cityoflondon.gov.uk
Golders Green tube.

## RICHMOND PARK

Deer can be seen all over the capital – in fact, photographers have even glimpsed urban herds making their way through suburban East London streets at night time – but nothing quite matches encountering them in the wilds of this 2,500-acre royal park. A legacy of Richmond Park's early life as a hunting area (and the long-time scourge of the area's dog walkers), the 630 free roaming Red and Fallow deer are easy enough to spot and chancing upon an idling stag on a misty morning is a guaranteed jaw-dropper for most kids. However, be aware that during rutting (September to October) and birthing season (May to July) it's even more crucial to stay at a safe distance.

---

Holly Lodge, TW10 5HS.
0300 061 2200
www.royalparks.org.uk
Richmond rail, tube and Overground.

## FREIGHTLINERS CITY FARM

Set back from Holloway Road and a quick hop from Upper Street's infinite distractions, this popular, mud-spattered community hub has location and history on its side. That name comes from the fact that, in its original location behind King's Cross station, the animals at Freightliners used to be housed in disused rail carriages (one of which is still on display for any tiny trainspotters). What's more – from the local honey in the farm shop to the straw bale walls of the café – there's a rustic, funsize feel to the place. And as well as some expected, exceptionally friendly animals (pigs, sheep, goats, ducks and a few cat interlopers) there are rarer beasts like the formidable Flemish Giant rabbits.

—

Sheringham Road, N7 8PF.
020 7609 0467
www.freightlinersfarm.org.uk
Highbury & Islington tube and Overground.

## RAINHAM MARSHES

A fertile home to wildlife just off the A13 may not sound promising, but the gritty surroundings – cars at the horizon, looming wind turbines and the distant tower of the Shard – only enhance the tranquility of this free bird reserve. Run by the RSPB and normally filled with serious-looking twitchers with expensive telescopes, Rainham Marshes is also great for kids. There's the wildlife, of course – which includes not just feathered friends but voles, fluttering butterflies, frogs, snakes and whirring crickets. Make your way up a winding pathway and there's a varied adventure playground complete with challenging climbing boulders for any easily-bored older kids. The café does great homemade scones and if you forget your binoculars (an essential for budding ornithologists) they can be hired from the shop.

——

New Tank Hill Road, Purfleet, Rainham,
South Ockenden, RM19 1SZ.
01708 899 840
www.rspb.org.uk
Purfleet rail.

## WOODBERRY WETLANDS

Bordered by high-rises and formed from a pair of nineteeth-century reservoirs, this 11-hectare Stoke Newington site – long a cult spot for in-the-know birdwatchers – is possibly the newest urban oasis in the capital. Walk through its artfully rusted metal entrance and you can't help but feel you've ventured through a secret portal. Reeds sway in the wind, birds (including kingfishers and reed warblers) skim the water and dragonflies buzz all the way along a route that's thankfully not too challenging for little legs. There are plenty of events held throughout the year (including bat nights for those brave enough to nudge bedtime a little later), nature-themed craft sessions for kids and the café – in a converted coal house – does a mean brunch.

—

Lordship Road, N16 5HQ.
020 8802 4573
www.woodberrywetlands.org.uk
Manor House tube.

## HANWELL ZOO

Spare a thought for West London parents who think a forbidding trip to London Zoo is the only way to see exotic animals. Tucked away in the patch of Ealing greenery locally known as the Bunny Park, this mini zoo (which began life as a home for unwanted pets and animals seized in customs) offers a free encounter with some unusual beasts. There are meerkats, butterflies, kune kune pigs, lemurs, marmosets – one of whom was liberated from a smuggler's trousers – and all manner of other inquisitive creatures to keep kids interested. In addition, friendly, knowledgeable staff are on hand to fill visitors in on each guest's unique story and the park has a fantastic maze to wander through on the way home.

—

Church Road, W7 3BP.
07803 454510
www.ealing.gov.uk
Hanwell rail.

# GIMME SHELTER

younger
Readers

# GIMME SHELTER

Parenthood brings out the amateur meteorologist in all of us.
Weather apps are consulted, clouds are watched, storm gods
are prayed to, all in the name of trying to avoid the feeling
of trapped delirium that occasionally accompanies rainy day
childcare. Of course, museums, swimming pools, soft play spots
and cinemas provide reliable cover, but — as befits a city that
sees its fair share of bucketing downpours — London has plenty
of sheltered sanctuaries offering something creative, active
or just enjoyably different to the usual wet weather haunts.
In fact, whether you're willing to spend money on an indoor snow
day or simply hunker down in a free reading nook, these places
are so good they'll make you wish for rain. Well, almost.

## THE IDOL

The standard soft play aesthetic of squishy primary colours is handed a thrilling twist at this permanent, explorable East London exhibit within a leisure centre. Created by Turner-nominated artist Marvin Gaye Chetwynd and inspired by a neolithic statue discovered in nearby marshland, The Idol is a sizeable indoor playground in the form of a hulking monochrome robot. The attention to detail is impressive – the Gothic chequerboard design even extends to the adjacent café – but there are familiar delights (slides, padded inclines, pools of white balls) to comfort any wary kids. Sessions are limited to two hours and can get busy. It's also worth noting that – despite the newborn-friendly high contrast design – there's not much here for the very young.

—

The Abbey Leisure Centre, Bobby Moore Way, Barking, IG11 7HW.
020 8227 3338
www.createlondon.org
Barking tube.

## NOVELTY AUTOMATION

Part interactive exhibit, part arcade, this Holborn hideout is truly one of the best kept secrets in the capital. Founded by engineer and cartoonist Tim Hunkin, it's essentially a collection of coin-operated machines that team eye-popping Wallace and Gromit-style gadgetry (the mechanical hands of the 'Autofrisk' will prompt yelps of delight) and Banksy-grade satire. Entry is free, and you can purchase tokens (at £1 each) to fly a paparazzi drone, enjoy a 'micro break' in a hyperactive armchair, grab coins with a 'money laundering crane' and much, much more. Be warned: it's more eccentric art installation than savvily designed play space – there are no toilets, for one thing – but it's a wonderfully weird place to spend an hour on bad weather days.

—

1A Princeton Street, WC1R 4AX.
No phone.
www.novelty-automation.com
Holborn tube.

## DISCOVER STORY CENTRE

Just a short walk from the gleaming byways of Westfield Stratford (a rainy day option in itself) lies a playspace with a difference. Creativity and care are evident in every corner of this indoor story trail, revamped in 2016 to encompass an adventure with steampunky, bird-like aliens named the Hootahs. It invites kids to concoct their own tales while exploring an indoor forest, a 'Lollipopter' and giant clouds over two detailed floors. Entry is moderately priced (the popular temporary exhibitions are included in the cost but time slots must be booked), there's a bookshop and sizeable, decent upstairs café. Also, if you get a sudden patch of good weather, the Story Garden – with its 'drivable' taxi and monster-themed climbing frame – is pretty special too.

----

383–387 High Street, E15 4QZ.
020 8536 5555
www.discover.org.uk
Stratford tube or Stratford High Street DLR.

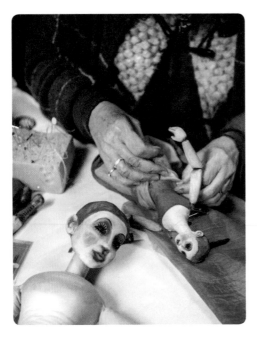

## LITTLE ANGEL THEATRE

Even in the age of rocketing commercial rent prices and e-petitions to save doomed independents, small family-run phenomena can still thrive. Founded in 1961 by John and Lyndie Wright – parents of Hollywood director Joe Wright – this 100-seater Islington puppet theatre and workshop still offers a gateway to a hidden world of marionettes, vibrant colour and quietly breathtaking stagecraft. Shows nicely balance the obscure with retellings of picture book blockbusters and, although it's best to book ahead, rainy summer days are generally quiet enough for walk-ins. Got a toddler who may struggle to sit through a whole show? The Sunday Crafternoon sessions introduce younger children to puppetry via a frenzy of card, pens and pots of glue.

—

14 Dagmar Passage, N1 2DN.
020 7226 1787
www.littleangeltheatre.com
Highbury and Islington or Angel tube.

## POLKA THEATRE

This utterly unique Wimbledon establishment – the first children's theatre in the UK when it opened in 1979 – is rightly known for challenging, innovative plays aimed at a younger audience. And the works in its main room and early years Adventure Theatre (which have, in the past, taken in futurism, kid-friendly shows inspired by the London riots, Shakespearean adaptations and even dramatised explorations of infant neuroscience) nail the trick of making performance palatable for the easily distracted. But even if you don't manage to get a ticket, the Polka is a studiously curated space for rain-soaked families. Its inviting, colourful foyer has rocking horses, toys and reading areas. Also, the café boasts ever-popular booths decked out to look like giant train carriages.

---

240 The Broadway, SW19 1SB.
020 8543 4888
www.polkatheatre.com
South Wimbledon tube.

## V&A MAKE IT WORKSHOPS

The Victoria & Albert Museum's sprawling mass of artistically significant artefacts may be more suited to older children, but its regular family experience sessions are classy affairs, run with patience, enthusiasm and an inclusive spirit. Communal art days for those with kids litter the capital and normally carry hefty price tags, but a ticket or two won't set you back too much here. For that, a working artist will take you and kids aged five to twelve through the creation of a themed work, ranging from decorative boxes for secrets to enjoyably messy clay-sculpting and teetering architectural challenges. Workshops can fill up quickly, though during school holidays the free drop-in Imagination Station gives you a similar feel with the added benefit of flexibility should you need to occupy the terminally cabin feverish on a stormy day.

—

Cromwell Road, SW7 2RL.
020 7942 2000
www.vam.ac.uk
South Kensington tube.

## KIDZANIA AT WESTFIELD

A city run by children could be a fragment from a dystopian novel – and it's the reality at this place: a mind-bendingly enjoyable mini metropolis tucked inside Westfield White City. Essentially, Kidzania offers children aged four to fourteen the chance to don scaled-down costumes for more than 60 adult jobs and experiences (think police officer, pilot, hotelier). The clincher is its scale and attention to detail. Indoor street signs give it the feel of a real, bustling town, activities don't skimp on technical info (junior surgeons can perform liver transplants) and kids can even earn pretend money to spend in the gift shop. Sessions run to four hours and electronic bracelets keep things safe and orderly. Pricey, exhausting, but unforgettable.

—

Westfield London, Ariel Way, W12 7GA.
0330 131 3333
www.london.kidzania.com
Shepherd's Bush tube.

## GREENWICH OBSERVATORY AND PLANETARIUM

Even on cold days you'll find a dedicated crowd of tourists straddling the meridian line in Greenwich park. But just around the corner, there's refuge from the elements within the suitably spacey jutting exterior of the Peter Harrison Planetarium. It's London's last working attraction of this kind, and bagging one of the gratifyingly comfy chairs in the 120-seater planetarium for a show – ranging from the lively audience interaction of

Meet the Neighbours to the cute Space Safari – is highly recommended. But few people know that the visitors centre is free to enter. And with its central hunk of 4.5-billion-year-old meteorite, it will keep any would-be astronomers happy for half an hour or so.

—

Blackheath Avenue, SE10 8XJ.
020 8312 6608
www.rmg.co.uk
Greenwich rail or Cutty Sark for Maritime Greenwich DLR.

## SOUTHBANK CENTRE –
## ROYAL FESTIVAL HALL

Spraying fountains – and an adjacent branch of burger-slinging kiddie-favourite Giraffe – make the Royal Festival Hall a regular summer stop-off for parents. But the carpeted expanse of the Southbank Centre's main hub is great for the colder months too. Hop in the giddy delight that is the singing lift (Martin Creed's audio installation Work No. 409) and hit the Saison Poetry Library, an undervisited marvel that has a small kids area with inviting bean bags. Outside the door, there's also a slightly bedraggled wooden structure (the Reading Den) that's festooned with books and chairs for a restful moment. Elsewhere, there's usually something to occupy you in the Foyer Spaces, be it interactive music sessions or the sight of street dancers practising their moves.

—

Belvedere Road, SE1 8XX.
020 7960 4200
www.southbankcentre.co.uk
Waterloo rail and tube.

## BARBICAN HIGHWALKS

With the Museum of London's City site, a library and of course an arts complex within scurrying distance, the area around the Barbican Centre isn't a bad place to head on an uninspired grey-skied day. Steeped in history (it was constructed in the Cripplegate area levelled by Luftwaffe bombing in 1940), the brutalist labyrinth that is the Barbican Estate boasts interconnected raised walkways that offer a strange, sheltered cocoon from the outside world and a good place to ride scooters or burn off steam following the directions painted on the floor. Furthermore, on most Sundays the conservatory – a jungle of towering palms, huddled cacti and kiddie-friendly carp ponds – is open to the public.

Silk Street, EC2Y 8DS.
020 7638 4141
www.barbican.org.uk
Barbican tube.

## CLIP N' CLIMB

Aspirant mountaineers who have conquered all their local climbing frames will get a kick out of this classy facility inside an ordinary-looking West London warehouse. Clip n' Climb is a world of riotous colour dominated by 20 pop art wall challenges of varying difficulty – including a face-to-face incline for competitive races and the Leap of Faith trapeze slide – plus three special attractions that carry an extra cost. Sessions (which always include a reassuringly thorough safety briefing) last 55 minutes and include harnesses to ease any jitters. It's suitable for anyone over the age of four but it's particularly good for adrenaline junkie older kids and, let's be honest, parents who can't resist having a go.

----

19 Michael Road, SW6 2ER.
020 7736 2271
www.clipnclimbchelsea.co.uk
Fulham Broadway tube.

## POTTERY CAFÉ

Kilns now lurk in all corners of the capital, but the Fulham branch of this ceramics studio has the feel of a true original. Set up in 1998 by Emma Bridgewater, patron saint of every middle class mug tree, it's nestled next to her persistently popular pottery shop. It is perhaps smaller than rival spaces, but that only adds to the bustle and cosy bonhomie as staff help pick out paintable plates, mugs and piggy banks before hopping behind the counter to make coffees and hot chocolates. Be warned: prices are very much in line with the well-heeled area (the same goes for the Battersea branch). But as a relaxing balm on a day when playgrounds and parks are off limits, it always delivers.

—

735 Fulham Road, SW6 5UL.
020 7736 2157
www.pottery-cafe.com
Parsons Green tube.
**BRANCHES:** Battersea SW11 6QB.

## THE BEES KNEES AT BATTERSEA ARTS CENTRE

South-West London has its very own phoenix in the form of the Battersea Arts Centre. Partially burnt down in 2015, it is rising once more (with a rebuilt version of its Grand Hall) thanks to donations from a public campaign that raised more than £50,000. One innovation that survived the flames is this inspired, popular indoor play space of rolling hills covered in felt grass, scattered toys and cosy cushions. Cheap to enter and designed with toddlers in mind, it's all the better for being hand painted and completely bespoke. It also has a café across the foyer – complete with hulking almond croissants – which adds the appealing proposition of a warm place for parents to cradle a well-earned cup of coffee.

—

Lavender Hill, SW11 5TN.
020 7223 2223
www.bac.org.uk
Clapham Junction rail and Overground.

## PUPPET BARGE THEATRE

There's a double hit of kid-pleasing rainy day distraction at this Little Venice barge-cum-marionette-performance space. Salvaged from a London boatyard by founders Gren Middleton and Juliet Rogers, and moored in the canal near Maida Vale since 1982, its unmistakable yellow and red canopy can be seen here between October and July (it floats down to Richmond for a late summer season in August). Creaking along the gangway into its 55-seat theatre – complete with dinky refreshment area and all important heating – is a magical experience worth the slight panic that accompanies any activity that requires your professional squirmers to sit still. Intervals help, and it's surprisingly spacious, but it's still probably best for those who have seen a few plays before.

---

35 Blomfield Road, W9 2PF.
020 7249 6876
www.puppetbarge.com
Warwick Avenue tube.

## THE SNOW CENTRE

When faced with teeth-chattering temperatures, most Londoners cuddle the nearest radiator, but there's something to be said for meeting Alpine weather with Alpine entertainment. Positioned just outside the M25 (and an easy 30-minute train journey from London Euston), this Hemel Hempstead hit is effectively a giant fridge with a 160-metre main slope of real snow. It's a regular stop for experienced skiers and snowboarders honing tricks, but there's also a separate learning area and on weekends kids as young as two can get a taste of the white stuff in the Snow Garden. A proper lift pass or lessons can be pricey, though equipment hire is included, sledding sessions are cheaper and there's an authentic après bar for a restorative hot chocolate afterwards.

—

St Albans Hill, Hemel Hempstead, Hertfordshire, HP3 9NH.
0344 770 7227
www.thesnowcentre.com
Hemel Hempstead or Apsley rail.

## BIG FISH LITTLE FISH

The very idea of a 'family rave' may still prompt sniggering from sceptics, but this roaming collective have done their bit to spread the gospel about afternoon parties with tunes to please the grown-ups and sensory distractions for under-age revellers. An eye for detail (glitter cannons, glow sticks, an art wall and a squeal-inducing finale with an unfurled giant canopy), quality DJs and attention-grabbing themes help Big Fish Little Fish stand out in an increasingly crowded market. Plus one of the joys of these events is that they work on multiple levels. Parents get stuck into drinks, older pop-obsessed kids run through coordinated moves and toddlers tear around amid the flashing lights.

—

Various locations.
07956 884530
www.bigfishlittlefishevents.co.uk

## ARTSDEPOT

Acting as a lone bulwark of culture amid the shops and idling buses on Finchley's Tally Ho Corner, this hub frequently hosts an appealing programme of family-ready shows in its two theatres. The regular appearances by Comedy Club 4 Kids – an enjoyably raucous but decidedly clean afternoon of non-patronising laughs from touring stand-ups – are worth keeping an eye out for. And, as with most arts spaces, there's lots of free indoor fun on offer during chilly months. Those with pre-schoolers should head for Playdepot, a woodland-themed area with giant foam building blocks, books and the requisite café for the grown-ups. Best of all, unlike a lot of soft play, there's no charge to enter.

---

5 Nether Street, N12 0GA.
020 8369 5454
www.artsdepot.co.uk
West Finchley tube.

## PICKLED PEPPER BOOKS

A quiet corner in a thoughtfully arranged children's book section can be just the tonic in times of lashing sideways rain, and this colourful institution deep in Crouch End's Bugaboo belt is truly something special. Lovingly run by husband and wife Urmi Merchant and Steven Pryse – and cheekily billed as for 'kids and their grown-ups' – Pickled Pepper Books nails that trick of allying a busy calendar of events (frequently involving readings from the rock stars of the children's literature world) with an airy, welcoming space. There are after-school reading clubs for older bibliophiles and the presence of a small café invites you to linger and lose an hour or two without fear of purchase pressure.

—

10 Middle Lane, N8 8PL.
020 3632 0823
www.pickledpepperbooks.co.uk
Hornsey rail.

# TEENAGE KICKS

# TEENAGE KICKS

Ah, teenagers. All stereotypes contain a crumb of truth and even easygoing older kids can succumb to the trademark traits – eyes fixed on a smartphone, lip curled in disgust, shoulders disdainfully hunched – that can make catering for them maddeningly difficult. And, of course, what may be heaven for one over-12 is just as likely to be hell for another. But don't throw in the towel and trudge defeatedly to the nearest shopping centre quite yet. From grown-up galleries and edible craft sessions to trampoline training and tea in a neon wonderland, it's not impossible to find London attractions that are exhilarating, adult and just downright fun enough to impress this notoriously picky crowd.

## GO APE

A longtime favourite of stag and hen parties, this national chain of treetop adventure centres also provide a smart pick for families with a taste for (reassuringly harnessed) daredevilry. In fact, this Battersea branch is the highest in the country, making up for a lack of forest-roaming space with a tightly packed circuit of wobbly walkways, 'flying carpets' and zip lines. Entry is far from cheap, but it's a thrilling afternoon out — particularly on blustery days — that always engenders wide grins and adrenalin-pumping camaraderie. Helpfully, there are three tiers of difficulty depending on the bravery of your kids and, if anyone really loses their nerve, there's mini golf and pizzas down on the bottom floor.

—

Albert Bridge Road, SW11 4NJ.
0333 433 0983
www.goape.co.uk
Battersea Park rail and Overground.

## ◄ DRAUGHTS

Not all of London's feted novelty establishments
are suitable for children (frustatingly, the presence
of booze means most video game bars are
adults-only). Luckily, this Haggerston board game
café – the first of its kind in the capital – extends
a pleasingly nerdy welcome to all ages. More
than 600 rainy day classics are available from the
library (ranging from Monopoly and The Game of
Life to complex modern hits like The Settlers of
Catan and A Game of Thrones: The Board Game).
A small entry on the door gets you unlimited
play at one of the cleverly designed tables. Chirpy,
knowledgable staff – sorry, 'game gurus' – are
on hand to explain any tricky rules and mediate
the inevitable family squabbles. Cheese and meat
boards are on hand if you work up an appetite.

----

337 Acton Mews, E8 4EA.
020 7254 1572
www.draughtslondon.com
Haggerston Overground.

## JURASSIC ENCOUNTER ADVENTURE GOLF

South London clearly has a thing for giant
prehistoric statues. Ten miles away from the
Victorian behemoths in Crystal Palace Park (see
page 16), this roadside New Malden attraction
turns mini golf and animatronic dinosaurs into
unlikely bedfellows. A 'what is that?' fixture for
those whizzing down the A3, Jurassic Encounter is
an 18-hole course of putting challenges peppered
with crashed vehicles, brightly coloured waterfalls
and nine near-lifesize moving dinosaurs. It's
decently priced and can cater to a mixed-age
group – the young and easily distracted can marvel
at the lurking velociraptors and snapping T-Rex
while teenagers get fiercely competitive as they
drink in the kitschy, holiday park fun.

----

Beverley Way, KT3 4PH.
020 8949 9200
www.jurassicencounter.com
New Malden or Raynes Park rail.

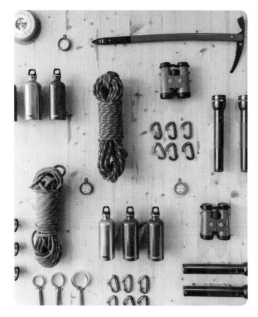 

## UP AT THE O2

The former Millennium Dome's cultural rehabilitation remains one of the most surprising success stories in the capital. And now, even clambering over its giant tent-like exterior has become an alternative family adventure. This bit of urban exploration – taking you up a slightly bouncy blue walkway to the summit and over – is very much worth the starting £28 fee, but do note: once you've stopped laughing at each other's Top Gun-style jumpsuits, the first portion of the harnessed expedition is pretty steep. Especially in a crosswind. But safety and inclusiveness is always paramount (you're accompanied by conscientious guides and the 16-strong group stays together), and the surprisingly tough moments will play well with youngsters yearning for something that feels reassuringly grown up.

———

Peninsula Square, SE10 0DX.
020 8463 2000
www.theo2.co.uk
North Greenwich tube.

## OXYGEN FREEJUMPING

Whether it's adult ball pools or cereal cafés, the capital's ever-expanding stable of kidult entertainment options aren't going anywhere anytime soon. And few places capture this blurring of the generational lines like this frenzied North Acton trampolining space. All ages (and that includes excitable parents or serious fitness addicts) are welcomed within this Tardis-like warehouse of 150 connected yellow-trim trampolines, airbags and other Gladiator-style obstacles. Free-jumping sessions are a fairly priced opportunity to dabble in gravity-defiance for an hour, but most teenagers will probably be up for events including bouncing dodgeball, freerunning classes and – for particularly hardy parental chaperones – Oxygen Project nights that feature games, disco lights and ear-splitting tunes spun by a live DJ.

——

15 Vision Industrial Park, Kendal Avenue, W3 0AF.
020 3846 1386
www.oxygenfreejumping.co.uk
West Acton tube.

## BISCUITEERS

Any kid who gets a kick out of the icing-based peril on The Great British Bake Off will lap up a visit to one of Biscuiteers' handsome boutiques in the suitably chic pockets of Notting Hill and Battersea. Firstly, there's the shop and café area, with brimming shelves of hand baked and iced luxury biscuits in all manner of creative shapes and seasonal varieties (edible high heels, anyone?), as well as aproned staff primed to send coffees, cakes and even milkshakes your way. The real draw here is the drop-in decorating area, though. For £15 kids are let loose with a box of freshly baked biccies and piping bottles brimming with colourful icings to create their own gift box of goodies or, inevitably, something to devour on the way home.

—

194 Kensington Park Road, W11 2ES.
020 7727 8096
www.biscuiteers.com
Ladbroke Grove tube.
**BRANCHES:** Battersea SW11 1NG.

## CLUEQUEST

Even the most biddable teenagers may take some convincing as you lead them towards an unassuming wooden door and explain that you're paying to enter a closed room. Nonetheless, this live escape game – imported from Hungary by ever-beaming hosts the Papp brothers – is one of London's most unusual and innovative experiences. Teams of three to five are challenged to solve a series of fiendish puzzles in order to escape a succession of secured spaces in under 60 minutes. There are three infectiously goofy games (ranging from spy-themed PLAN52 to sci-fi-tinged Revenge of the Sheep), dramatic music and ticking clocks crank up the tension as you fumble with padlocks, and a leaderboard gives it all a competitive edge.

----

169-171 Caledonian Road, N1 0SL.
07770 071 577
www.cluequest.co.uk
King's Cross St Pancras rail and tube.

## CAPITAL KARTS

Most teenagers will reach a stage where they're throwing longing glances at their parent's car keys. Believe it or not, there's a rooftop driving school for under-17s in Brent Cross. For a more exhilarating blast of miniature petrol headed action, however, take them to this go kart circuit on the Essex-borders. What Capital Karts lacks in looks (the hangar-like facility is perched on the edge of the A13 and decked out in gritty black and red), it more than makes up for in size, with its 1,050 metres of winding turns forming Britain's longest indoor track. Kids aged 12 and over can all suit up for a spin, while under-15s get special £30 Sunday morning sessions.

—

Unit 1, Rippleside, IG11 0RJ.
020 7100 4412
www.capitalkarts.com
Upney or Becontree tube.

## ALL STAR LANES

The traditional family trip to the bowling alley – with its ancient arcade machines, grotty carpets and cheapo chicken dippers (not to mention smelly shoes) – gets a hell of a high-end twist at this stable of boutique tenpin emporiums. Having opened their flagship Holborn branch in 2006, All Star Lanes (alongside similarly pitched rivals Bloomsbury Bowling) were originators of the sort of classily reconfigured play palaces that paved the way for London's ping pong bars and luxe-darts establishments. The blaring music, moody lighting and glossy 1950s styling plays well with over-12s, and then there's the food and drink. Whichever venue you go for (the original, Brick Lane, Bayswater or Stratford) a towering chocolate, caramel, peanut butter and banana shake is basically non-negotiable (while kitsch cocktails will please the grown-ups).

———

Victoria Place, Bloomsbury Place, WC1B 4DA.
020 7025 2676
www.allstarlanes.co.uk
Holborn tube.
**BRANCHES:** Bayswater W2 4DB; Brick Lane E1 6QL; Stratford E20 1ET.

## THE CHAINSTORE PARKOUR ACADEMY

Baggy-trousered types leaping gracefully over bollards and ledges have been a regular sight in the capital for at least the past decade. And now free runners have a place to practise (without angering security guards) at this hidden hub over the river from The O2. Acting as a base for the Parkour Generations collective, it's a purpose-built indoor urban jungle of scaffolding, ladders, wooden blocks and other obstacles that includes an observation deck for parents that may not think their creaky knees are up to it. There are fitness classes, drop-in sessions and dedicated Youth Academy days where experts justify the reasonable entry fee with enthusiastic, safe instruction. It's a great active afternoon and nearby Fat Boy's Diner is the ultimate post-parkour pit stop.

—

Trinity Buoy Wharf, 64 Orchard Place, E14 0JY.
020 3651 3364
www.parkourgenerations.com
Royal Victoria DLR.

## LEE VALLEY WHITE WATER CENTRE

Alongside the twisted form of Anish Kapoor's ArcelorMittal Orbit (see page 58), one of the best toys left behind after The London 2012 Summer Olympics may be this giant, artificial riverbed. For adrenalin-loving over-14s, the temptation to hop in a group raft and take on the sodden dips and turns of the full course will prove strong. But be warned: a day here can be just as exhausting as it is exhilarating. There's a thorough safety briefing, an icy dip to prove your proficiency in the water and a kindly drill sergeant of an instructor bellowing orders throughout. Those after something easier (or under-14s) can make a splash in the smaller Legacy Loop area on a Hydrospeed board or in a Hot Dog canoe, and even younger ones can stomp around in the sand in the designated beach area.

—

Station Road, Waltham Cross, Hertfordshire, EN9 1AB.
0300 003 0616
www.gowhitewater.co.uk
Waltham Cross or Cheshunt rail.

## BUNKER 51

What better way to get a pack of teenagers to put away their phones than a spot of post-apocalyptic warfare? Laser tag – that mainstay of suburban 1990s kids everywhere – gets a modern reboot at this subterranean playscape in the shadow of the Thames Barrier. Firing lasers through the atmospheric warrens of the bunker (which comes complete with murky flashing lights, scramble nets, oil drums and other pieces of authentically dystopian set dressing) will be enough for some,

but the big draw here, beyond the zombie experience days, is the indoor paintball that's only available for over-12s. Thankfully, the impact of the pellets is reassuringly soft and for £35 you're kitted out with a protective face mask and special ops jumpsuit.

—

3 Herringham Road, SE7 8NJ.
0330 333 8085
www.ultimaterecreation.co.uk
Charlton rail.

## THE WELLCOME COLLECTION

You won't get the usual logjam of excitable primary school visitors at this decidedly grown-up and enchantingly weird vault of medical and scientific artefacts on Euston Road. Formed from the lifetime haul of late-Victorian pharmaceutical entrepreneur Henry Wellcome, there's a grisly eccentricity to the free permanent exhibitions, which include Napoleon's toothbrush, a grimacing Peruvian mummy and antique bellows used for administering resuscitative tobacco enemas. It's aimed at over-14s and very adult in some places – some parents may want to swerve the Japanese sex aids – but it's all underpinned by fascinating anthropological nuggets. There's a big, busy café, and it's the perfect spot for kids who think they know what to expect from a trip to the museum.

—

183 Euston Road, NW1 2BE.
020 7611 2222
www.wellcomecollection.org
Euston or Euston Square tube.

## STREET ART LONDON TOUR

Got a kid who knows their Banksy from their Ben Eine? Resist any grumbles about forking out to look at some drawing on a wall and sign up for one of these absorbing mobile introductions to the capital's street art. There's a two-hour meander around Shoreditch and Hackney Wick, or a longer four-hour tour you can do by bicycle for extra East London points. Also, your engaging guides more than justify the reasonable fee. They are experts with a knack for demystifying the different styles – ranging from Roa's giant wispy animals to Clet Abraham's manipulated stop signs – and close links to the underground artists in the world. Sure to earn you some parental cool points.

—

Various locations.

No phone.

www.streetartlondon.co.uk/tours

Old Street tube.

## GOD'S OWN JUNKYARD

London meets Las Vegas at this glowing railside gallery in Walthamstow. Formed from the life work of late neon artist Chris Bracey and other reclaimed pieces, it's a truly unique jumble of signs from pawn shops, dive bars, films, photo shoots and disreputable Soho establishments. Walking into this lock-up on an unassuming industrial estate – past the brightly coloured model cow at the door – is a truly breathtaking experience, and the throbbing colours of the interior will play very well with any youngsters who have a taste for hip design (and, to be honest, covetable selfie backgrounds). It's free to enter, open from Friday to Sunday and there's a café – the excellently named Rolling Scones – which may be one of the capital's coolest spots to sip on a coffee.

----

Unit 12, Ravenswood Industrial Estate,
Shernhall Street, E17 9HQ.
020 8521 8066
www.godsownjunkyard.co.uk
Walthamstow Central tube and Overground
or Wood Street rail and Overground.

## THAMES RIB EXPERIENCE

Many an unprepared tourist has been taken aback by the neck-whipping speed of a trip on the Thames Clipper but, frankly, that's like a pedalo ride compared to this high velocity spin up the river. Ribs (rigid-inflatable boats) are those spy-worthy dinghies capable of up to 40mph and here, after donning a lifejacket, you clamber into a black and yellow beast for a breathless tour of London. It's not cheap (adult tickets for the 20-minute package around Tower Bridge are £24.50), but each trip is run with real wit – the James Bond theme blares out of the speakers as you pass a 007 location – and nothing tops clinging on while the capital's most iconic landmarks fly by.

---

Victoria Embankment, WC2N 6NU.
020 3613 2345
www.thamesribexperience.com
Embankment tube.

## BAYSIXTY6

London's grafitti-daubed South Bank undercroft – saved from closure by the public in 2014 – may be a gritty cultural icon but it can be a foreboding place for beginner skateboarders. Better to take them to this cavernous, sheltered skatepark under the Westway that pairs everything your nascent kick flippers or scooter riders could need (plentiful ramps, a bowl, lockers, an onsite skate shop, parent-pleasing safety equipment) with an inclusive atmosphere. There's a dedicated area for beginners, weekend mornings for novices, fairly priced entry – a session starts from just £2 for the under-16s After School Club – and equality is encouraged with monthly girls-only nights. They even hire boards, should any parents (perhaps unwisely) feel the need to roll back the years.

—

Acklam Road, W10 5YU.
No phone.
www.baysixty6.com
Westbourne Park tube.

# CAFÉS & RESTAURANTS

# CAFÉS & RESTAURANTS

The issue of unleashing young children on otherwise tranquil cafés and restaurants can be a thorny one. But just because you don't want to endure kid-phobic fellow diners tutting loudly doesn't necessarily mean you desire a lifetime of the same chips-with-everything screaming emporiums. Luckily, the capital is now packed with all sorts of innovative compromises that include Berlin-style kindercafés, buzzy diners and even terrific chains. Then there's the delicate business of pubs. Those after a quiet pint may bemoan the days when children were left outside with just a lowered car window and a bag of crisps for company, but some of London's taverns get the balancing act of boozers and buggies just right, and you'll find them here.

## CHIEF COFFEE

Let's hear it for café owners willing to indulge their secret passions. Chief Coffee's proprietor Sam McCourt is as obsessed with vintage arcade ephemera as he is with perfectly roasted beans, and his twin obsessions are both indulged in the form of London's first hybrid espresso room and pinball lounge. Upstairs you'll find a veritable dreamland for coffee nerds, featuring a custom copper brew station, high-grade sandwiches and expertly made cups of black gold from Workshop and Drop. While downstairs there's a rotating collection of pinball machines (both contemporary and vintage) ready to keep tiny flipper fingers busy and the very young transfixed by the flashing lights. Utterly unique and elegantly designed, it's a neon paradise that also pays host to regular competitions.

—

Turnham Green Terrace Mews, W4 1QU.
020 8994 0636
www.chief-coffee.com
Turnham Green tube.

## TOCONOCO

Bored of the same variations on baked beans and crustless sandwiches? This Japanese café may just offer salvation for understimulated family palates. Tucked away in a canalside development near Kingsland Road's hipster thoroughfare, Toconoco (which loosely translates as 'kids on the floor') is a fiercely child-friendly local secret with an astroturfed play area brimming with blocks, vehicles and elegant wooden toys. Food is simple and authentically cooked. There's a single daily lunch special – think vegetable omelette, beef chilli or a fragrant tinfoil parcel of grilled white fish with ponzu sauce – alongside interesting twists on brunch staples (wasabi and avocado on toast can be made without the fiery kick for younger diners) and a striking, squidgy wedge of black sesame cheesecake. Truly special.

---

Unit A, 28 Hertford Road, N1 5QT.
020 7249 8394
www.toconoco.com
Haggerston Overground.

## TRAMSHED

Mark Hix's chicken and steak joint was ahead of the minimalist menu curve when it swaggered into Shoreditch in 2012, and it's still a sanctuary for savvy parents. The venue should engender awestruck silence – the high-ceilinged former tramway generator building is dominated by Damien Hirst's specially commissioned work 'Cock and Bull' – and Hix is a master of welcoming families. As at his other establishments, kids under ten eat free at certain times and there's a colouring-in competition that feels apt in a space that doubles as a gallery. The food offering has swelled recently to include supersized puddings, but meat-eaters should go for the stalwart attraction: salt-chamber aged beef or barn-reared chicken served with a moat of crispy fries.

—

32 Rivington Street, EC2A 3LX.
020 7749 0478
www.hixrestaurants.co.uk
Old Street tube or Shoreditch High Street Overground.

## TOM'S KITCHEN

If you emerge from one of South Kensington's ever-busy museums with the haunted gaze of a war veteran, an early dinner at Tom Aikens's nearby Chelsea restaurant should set you right. Now installed in various prime pieces of London real estate – Somerset House, Canary Wharf, a converted corner of HMS Belfast – the original Tom's Kitchen nails the trick of understated kid-friendliness (ample buggy room, crayons and paper) in an airy, clatteringly atmospheric space. The menu is full of fairly-priced, culinary hugs too. Highlights for kids include tangy tomato pasta and cheese, fish nuggets and fruit skewers, while adults should avail themselves of the peerless fish pie or a buttery brunchtime slab of brioche French toast. Pretty much unbeatable.

—

27 Cale Street, SW3 3QP.
020 7349 0202
www.tomskitchen.co.uk
South Kensington or Sloane Square tube.
**BRANCHES**: Canary Wharf E14 4HD;
Somerset House WC2R 1LA; St Katharine's
Dock E1W 1AZ; HMS Belfast SE1 2JH.

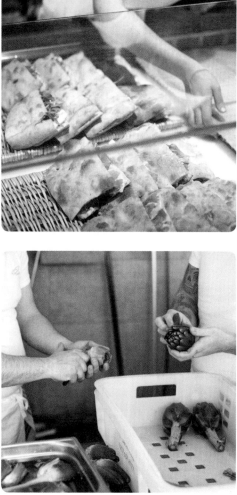

## ◄ PRINCI

The chaos visible through the wide windows of this Wardour Street bakery will be a welcome sight to parents eager to avoid disapproving tuts from kid-free neighbouring tables. Bustling, forgivingly noisy and crisply designed, this sole London outpost of the Milanese chain has gone from strength to strength since it was launched by Wagamama mastermind Alan Yau in 2008. And there's bound to be something on the sprawling menu of doughy pizzas, hefty focaccia sandwiches, lasagne, pastries and more that will get a member of your brood salivating. Yes, it's not the cheapest and the self-service ordering system in the main area can test childish patience but as a speedy, atmospheric lunch in the heart of the West End it's hard to top.

—

135 Wardour Street, W1F 0UT.
020 7478 8888
www.princi.com
Tottenham Court Road or Oxford Circus tube.

## ELECTRIC DINER

Tinned hotdogs, powdered milkshake, baskets of limp, soggy chips – the concept of the American diner has been brutalised on occasion by us Brits, but this lively Portobello Road favourite is pure class. Expect to find plenty of immaculately turned-out young families spilling in from Notting Hill or members-only Kids Club screenings at the adjacent Electric Cinema to commandeer a bright red booth and feast on kids options like flat iron chicken, salmon and broccoli and veggie taglioni. There's a noisy, grown-up buzz to the place that older kids will appreciate and, while exquisite negronis and draught craft beer will tease a grateful smile from adults, a complimentary scoop of ice cream does the same for younger guests.

—

191 Portobello Road, W11 2ED.
020 7908 9696
www.electricdiner.com
Ladbroke Grove tube.

## CEREAL KILLER CAFÉ

What could be better for older kids than a bowl of cereal for lunch? This hipsterfied celebration of sugary breakfast items has surfed a storm of anti-gentrification animosity (it was targeted by protesters in 2015) to become an infectiously daft culinary phenomenon that still draws crowds in Brick Lane and Camden. Okay, no one is suggesting that Cereal Killer's collection of more than 120 imported treats – including Australian Milo, US Froot Loops and maple bacon Pop Tarts – should be the basis of a balanced diet but there's a lively, technicolour anarchy to the place. Parents can squeal at the 1990s ephemera and those supposedly contentious mark-ups (£4 for a 'Chocopottomus' cocktail) aren't that far north of what plenty would spend on a large latte.

—

139 Brick Lane, E1 6SB.
020 3601 9100
www.cerealkillercafe.co.uk
Shoreditch High Street Overground.
**BRANCHES:** Camden NW1 8AH.

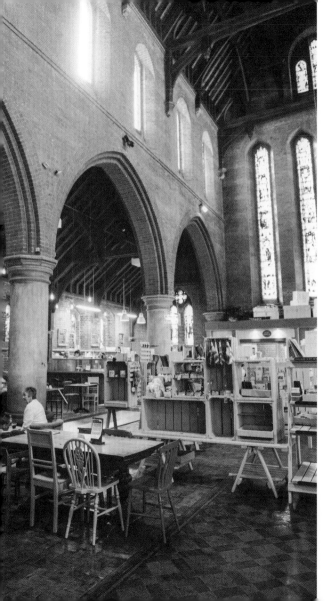

### SANCTUARY CAFÉ

Don't be fooled by the unassuming red brick exterior, St James Church in West Hampstead is not your average functioning house of worship. Follow the steady cavalcade of buggies inside and, as well as a post office, you'll find a godsend of a café and soft play area. Under a cool neon sign young, unflappable staff serve up coffee, plastic plates of kiddie food (the usual safe bets plus 'picky bits' platters and Nutella-smeared crackers) and truly excellent homemade treats in an atmosphere that balances tranquility (see the stained glass windows and upcycled pew tables) with tyke-friendly pandemonium. The fact that all profits go to the in-house Sheriff Centre charity is just the icing on the impeccably baked carrot cake.

—

St James Church, Sheriff Road, NW6 2AP.
020 7625 1184
www.thesheriffcentre.co.uk
West Hampstead tube.

## THE RIVINGTON

If the concept of 'kids eat free' conjures visions of grim roadside carveries and plates of lukewarm turkey drummers, this classy family brasserie should offer a corrective. Yes, in its South London and East London branches small people get a complimentary meal at certain times (and ninja-like staff are ever-primed with crayons and highchairs) but there's equally lots for parents to savour here. The seasonal all-day menu of British classics (think girolles on toast, Scotch eggs to snack on, homemade fish fingers, creamy barley risotto) is faultless, and there's a 130-bottle gin list to entice any drinkers. The Greenwich branch – with its boat-themed terrace – forms a particularly good one-two with the Maritime Museum (see page 43) or Cutty Sark.

---

178 Greenwich High Road, SE10 8NN.
020 8293 9270
www.rivingtongrill.co.uk
Greenwich rail and DLR.
**BRANCHES:** Shoreditch EC2A 3DZ.

## VICO

Chains have a stranglehold on central London when it comes to families. And that's fine in most cases but, occasionally, you want a break from being processed by the high street regulars. This bustling Italian on a coveted corner in Cambridge Circus offers something different but equally fail-safe. There's no specific kids menu but Vico's Lazio-influenced small plates – skewers of delicately spiced sausage, pizzas, moreish courgette chips, crispy arancini balls – play well with tiny bellies and the piazza-themed room is the real star here. There's a central fountain that's great for fidgety kids and nestled in the corner is a dedicated stand from London gelato masters Gelupo. A classier way to bribe them with ice cream.

1 Cambridge Circus, Seven Dials, WC2H 8PA.
020 7379 0303
www.eatvico.com
Leicester Square tube.

## BEAR + WOLF

Macbook-tapping freelancers and harried childcarers somehow coexist at this lively Tufnell Park spot. Similar in format to Berlin's chic kindercafés, it was a longtime passion project for local dad Matthew Neel and there are all manner of thoughtful touches for toddler-wranglers in particular (a buggy parking area, space-saving clamp-on high chairs, a bottomless cereal bowl on the kids menu) balanced with a pleasingly cool space. The biggest parental draw here, however, is the Cubroom: a huge, orderly play area crammed with toys, vehicles and books. There's a pocket garden out back and the brunch-themed all day menu — with everything-but-the-kitchen-sink breakfast rolls and shepherds pie for grown-ups and little ones — is dynamite.

---

153 Fortress Road, NW5 2HR.
020 3601 1900
www.bearandwolfcafe.com
Tufnell Park tube.

BUGGY PARKING

· JUICES & SMOOTHIES
'ALL DAY BREAKFAST' → BANANA · DATES · OATS $ YOGH...
'BREAKFAST BERRY' → FROZEN BERRIES · DATES $ YOG...
ORANGE · THAI BASIL · FROZEN STRAWBERRIES $ GINGER...
'MANGO/LASSI' FROZEN MANGO · COCONUTWATER · BANANA · YOGHU...
APPLE · PEAR · CARROT · FENNEL $ GINGER ·
FROZEN MANGO · APPLE $ MINT ·
BEETROOT · APPLE · CARROT · GINGER $ MINT ·
FROZEN SUMMER BERRIES · ORANGE · MINT $ AGAVE ·
'THE MEAL IN A GLASS' → BANANA · AVOCADO · YOGHURT · MILK · V...
'THE GREEN ONE' → APPLE · PEAR · CUCUMBER · CELERY · LIME · SP...
KIDS JUICES ALSO AVAILABLE!!!
# PLEASE FOLLOW US ON TWITTER @ BE...

## HUGGLE

There's more than a hint of Scandinavian chic to this beautifully designed shop-cum-café. Nestled in an unremarkable development a short stroll from the high-walled property porn of Swiss Cottage, it combines an upscale children's store with a community space and a dinky place for a coffee and a slice of cake. The devil is in the details here – from a clever buggy park and a toddler-friendly lowered toilet to a toy train set – and while Huggle is definitely more of a retail space (specialising in top-of-the-range pushchairs and kid-friendly furniture) than somewhere to meet friends for a prolonged catch-up, it turns tracking down products for your own kids or hunting presents for the inevitable pile-up of baby birthdays into a singularly pleasurable experience.

----

8-10 Winchester Road, NW3 3NT.
020 3468 0352
www.huggle.co.uk
Swiss Cottage tube.

## BANNER'S ▶

A welly boot full of crayons, the crammed pinboard of local information, a bill that comes in a hollowed-out coconut with a handful of jelly beans – it's the little touches that make this 25-year-old Crouch End veteran such a resounding (and bracingly popular) hit. Festooned with rock memorabilia – and alledgedly once visited by Bob Dylan – it's very much worth the unavoidable weekend bunfight for a table. The weighty all-day menu overflows with Caribbean-influenced, mega-portioned masterstrokes (fiery breakfast potatoes, deftly spiced jerk chicken burger, meat-free '4 Alarm' chilli) and boasts a sizeable children's section that features a semi-legendary pile of mash, baked beans and cheese called 'Tiny Meal'. Book ahead and be prepared to over-order.

----

21 Park Road, N8 8TE.
020 8348 2930
www.bannersrestaurant.com
Highgate tube or Crouch Hill Overground.

## MAMMA DOUGH

Swing by the Honor Oak branch of this small sourdough pizza chain for an early dinner and you'd be forgiven for thinking a mammoth children's party was underway. This restaurant in a converted bank – alongside its sibling outposts in Peckham and Brixton – has become a serious hit with local families so you'd be advised to book ahead. Snag a table amid the tomato can plant pots and you're in for a reliable treat. There are highchairs, changing facilities and incredibly cheap kid-size options of the expertly blistered doughy regulars. Specials impress (think pepperoni, pesto drizzle and olives) and the speed of service is great for the impatient. Parents and older kids should also make a beeline for the spiky homemade ginger ale.

----

76–78 Honor Oak Park, SE23 1DY.
020 8699 5196
www.mammadough.co.uk
Honor Oak Park Overground.
**BRANCHES:** Brixton SW9 8QH,
Peckham SE15 2ND.

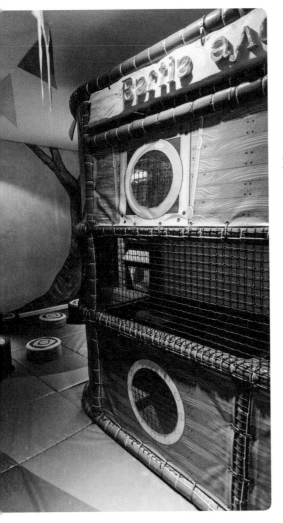

## BERTIE AND BOO ADVENTURE ISLAND

The balance of power is very much tipped in favour of the under-5s at this South London-based cluster of brightly coloured, consistently popular play cafés. The original coffee shop – with its outdoor deckchairs, sprinkle-topped babyccinos and a vintage car that's begging to be clambered on – is a terrific stop-off, perfect for watching Balham's brunch-loving hordes go by. But it's the other nearby stop-offs (the fairly priced Adventure Island soft play and a Clapham restaurant with padded mayhem zone) that provide the most entertainment on uninspired afternoons. Yes, it can feel like trespassing on a CBeebies set, but it's assembled with the care you'd expect from owners who run children's parties. And the Kinder Bueno milkshakes are seriously good.

—

205–207 Balham High Road, SW17 7BQ.
020 3620 1785
www.bertieandboo.com
Balham rail or tube.
**BRANCHES:** Balham SW12 9BW, Clapham SW11 6QF.

## HURWUNDEKI

Combining the none-more-East-London enterprises of a hip barbershop and Korean café, this Bethnal Green favourite also boasts a surprising third function: unlikely stop-off for inquisitive kids. The captivating outdoor space – a giant sandpit of mismatched furniture, junkyard curios and dilapidated toy animals – will be the chief draw for your small accomplices, but the dirt-cheap menu and superior Workshop coffee should keep you situated for some time. The MSG-free kitchen speedily churns out complex bowls of bibimbap, exemplary kimchi pancakes and crispy fried chicken strips that play well with most kids. Run with real love by local impresario (and dad of two) Ki-Chul Lee, it's an utterly inimitable magnet for parents after something different.

—

298–299 Cambridge Heath Road, E2 9HA.
020 7749 0638
www.hurwundeki.com
Cambridge Heath rail or Bethnal Green tube.

## THE SPOKE

This Holloway café-cum-pub may be cycle-themed but buggy pushers will be pleased to hear that four wheels are just as welcome as two. During the morning, plenty of prams crowd a handsomely mismatched interior – think old treacle tins, long wooden tables and shiny metro tiles – as local parents distract small folk with a bumper selection of toys in between mouthfuls of poached eggs with chilli avocado or jars of fruit-topped granola. Cherry-red cups of Union coffee hit the spot too, but this is very much an all-day space, and the cocktails, bottled craft beers and belting burgers (try the mouth-watering prawn po' boy sandwich) – not to mention the plentiful highchairs – make it perfect for an early evening tipple with tykes.

---

710 Holloway Road, N19 3NH.
020 7263 4445
www.thespokelondon.com
Upper Holloway Overground.

# KID-FRIENDLY PUBS

### THE ROSENDALE

From the weekend rotisserie chicken stall by the door to the pizza boards being hustled out of the kitchen, this West Dulwich mothership is a place that caters to a wide-ranging crowd. As is evident in the hordes of grateful mums and dads that descend here on sunny (and not so sunny) Saturdays and Sundays. The back garden area – an astroturfed and surprisingly serene jumble of Wendy Houses, toy vehicles and playground equipment – is undoubtedly what encourages people from miles away to make the pilgrimage. But the kitchen offering (especially the roast pork belly) is not be sniffed at, there are shrewdly curated local beers, small people can decorate their own dinky fairy cakes and table football will keep older children entertained.

—

65 Rosendale Road, SE21 8EZ.
020 8761 9008
www.therosendale.co.uk
West Dulwich rail.

## JAM CIRCUS

A short hop from the glittering post-war artefact that is The Rivoli Ballroom (the capital's only intact 1950s dance hall), this lively Brockley pub may lack a proper garden but it makes up for it with a clever concession to local parents. Once a week, and on occasional bank holidays, the snug area is given over to a pop-up soft play complete with giant padded slides, blocks and the usual frenzy of flung plastic balls to keep kids amused while their parents sup hoppy beers or glasses of wine. It's still worth a visit when the designated play zone isn't there, though. The back room has plenty of space, deep sofas and an old TV with a trunk of retro VHS tapes. A reasonably priced buffet also offers a more adventurous alternative to the standard kids' menu of beans and eggs on toast.

----

330–332 Brockley Road, SE4 2BT.
020 8692 3320
www.jamcircus.com
Brockley rail.

### THE OLD DAIRY

Life drawing, bring-your-own wine night, quizzes, invent-a-pie-filling competition – there's a lively 'try-anything' sense of fun and community to this old-fashioned Crouch Hill bar, and it all trickles down into a welcoming experience for families. Children get a print-out of a cow to colour in on arrival – a touch that's nicely suited to a Grade II-listed building that, as the name suggests, used to house a functioning creamery – and the kitchen balances safe bets for the kids with buccaneering gastropub twists for grown-ups. Make a beeline for the brightly coloured Chesterfield sofas and sample tempura courgette flowers, sea bream with sautéed fennel and a brownie-spiked sundae you may have to fight your offspring for.

—

1–3 Crouch Hill, N4 4AP.
020 7263 3337
www.theolddairyn4.co.uk
Crouch Hill rail.

## THE EAGLE

London's cramped streets and vertiginous rents don't always afford the room for the sort of sprawling beer gardens you find in the countryside. But this Shepherd's Bush favourite on the edge of Ravenscourt Park boasts one of the capital's best outdoor spaces out back, bestrewn with giant, colourful bean bags, cabana-style shaded areas and, inevitably, a regular supply of faintly manic sprinting kids. Thankfully, there's strength in parental numbers here and on pleasant summer days the high quotient of families tucking into winningly cooked stodge (including sausage and mash for kids and a vast chicken and mushroom pie for grown ups) happily share the space with pub regulars grabbing a pint or a Pimms. It's amazing what some sunshine can do.

—

215B Askew Road, W12 9AZ.
020 8746 0046
www.theeaglew12.co.uk
Goldhawk Road tube.

# THE CHAIN GANG:

- **Franco Manca**
  Rapid expansion hasn't hurt these sourdough pizza masters – originally based in Brixton Market – when it comes to quality. Kids portions aren't available but those Neapolitan-style crusts are cheap and generous.
  *www.francomanca.co.uk*

- **Wahaca**
  Great locations (the South Bank spot is a particular life-saver) and mellow mini tacos make this Mexican joint a winner. There's even free babyccinos and £1.20 ice cream.
  *www.wahaca.co.uk*

- **Byron**
  Kids can grab crayons or spot the hidden model cows while they wait for food at this upmarket burger chain. Mini patties come with cucumber and carrot sticks to keep things vaguely virtuous.
  *www.byronhamburgers.com*

- **Giraffe**
  Parental resistance is futile in the face of this family juggernaut's offering of balloons, miniature plastic giraffes and noisy, pint-sized mayhem. Slick and crowd-pleasing with a sprawling global menu.
  *www.giraffe.net*

- **Carluccio's**
  There's a warm Italian welcome for young pasta-slurpers at this stable of busy restaurants. The mini menu packs surprises (think Chicken Milanese with rosemary potatoes) and kids eat free with a paying adult.
  *www.carluccios.com*

- **Nando's**
  It's not all tongue-scorching peri peri. Little diners get a milder menu (although sharing an adult chicken is a juicier option) and a natural fruit ice lolly sweetens the deal.
  *www.nandos.co.uk*

- **Wagamama**
  Diddy plates of chicken katsu, cod cubes and grilled chicken noodles offer a good, fresh option for kids not opposed to a spot of culinary adventure. Always appealingly noisy, too.
  *www.nandos.co.uk*

- **Rainforest Café**
  A chain in a global sense (they have locations in Tokyo, Paris and the US), this animatronic wildlife-themed Piccadilly grotto may be expensive but it can't fail to please.
  *www.therainforestcafe.co.uk*

- **Jamie's Italian**
  Top of the line Stokke highchairs and retro ViewMaster toys add to the feel of considered care at Jamie Oliver's amped-up trattoria. Chicken lollipops and lip-smacking meatballs bolster the kids offering.
  *www.jamieoliver.com/italian*

- **Bill's**
  This collection of market-themed all day restaurants have come a long way from their humble beginnings in a Sussex greengrocer. Expect terrific macaroni and cheese and cracking cod fish fingers.
  *www.bills-website.co.uk*

HATFIEL

A413

Chesham

A41

115

A1(M)

66

M1

WATFORD

Borehamwood

HIGH
WYCOMBE

119

50

M40

34

A404

81

WEMBLEY

29

MAIDENHEAD

131

91

M4

20

Windsor

SEE PAGE 184

65

83

M4

TWICKENHAM

17

Egham

BRACKNELL

62

10

129

M3

A240

22

WOKING

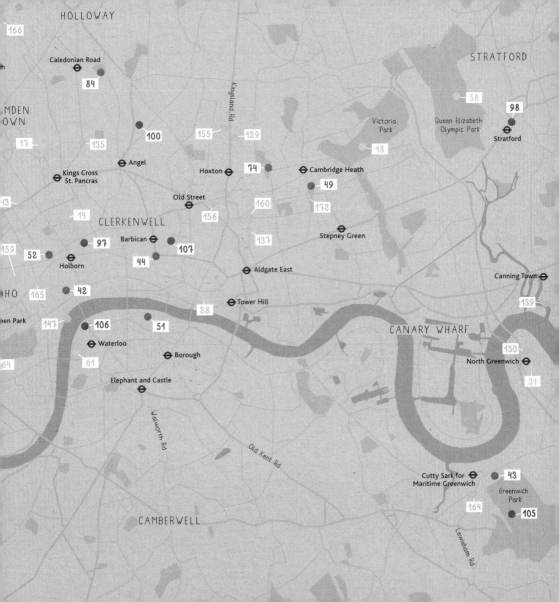

HOLLOWAY

166

STRATFORD

Caledonian Road

84

58

98

CAMDEN
TOWN

100

Victoria
Park

Queen Elizabeth
Olympic Park

Stratford

17

135

155

129

Angel

Kings Cross
St. Pancras

Hoxton

74

Cambridge Heath

18

49

13

Old Street

160

172

14

CLERKENWELL

156

Stepney Green

97

Barbican

137

159

52

107

Holborn

44

Aldgate East

Canning Town

42

165

Tower Hill

139

SOHO

28

CANARY WHARF

Green Park

147

106

51

130

64

Waterloo

North Greenwich

61

Borough

31

Elephant and Castle

Walworth Rd

Old Kent Rd

CAMBERWELL

Cutty Sark for
Maritime Greenwich

43

Greenwich
Park

164

105

Lewisham Rd

# INDEX

*Front cover: BaySixty6*
*Back cover: Victoria Park (top), Artsdepot*
*(bottom left), Crystal Palace Park (bottom right)*
*p1 Pottery Café; p2 Battersea Park Children's*
*Zoo; p3 Draughts; p4 Chainstore Parkour*
*Academy; p7 Lee Valley White Water Centre;*
*p8 All Star Lanes (top left), Lee Valley Park*
*Farms (top right), Freightliners City Farm*
*(bottom left), Oxygen Freejumping (bottom*
*right); p9 Southbank Centre; p180 Victoria Park;*
*p181 Lee Valley Park Farms (top left), Southbank*
*Centre (top right), Bertie Boo Adventure Island*
*(bottom left), Lee Valley Park Farms (bottom*
*right); p186-187 Brockwell Park; p191 Ruislip*
*Lido; p192 The Cartoon Museum*

Frances Lincoln Limited
An imprint of The Quarto Group
74–77 White Lion Street
London N1 9PF

*Family London*
Copyright © Frances Lincoln 2017
Text copyright © Jimi Famurewa 2017
Handwriting font copyright © Jenny Seddon 2017
Photographs copyright © Camille Mack 2017
Except the following: p20 © Gracian Doza; p21, p62 © Historic Royal
Palaces; p22 © Hobbledown; p42 top © Alamy/Greg Balfour Evans;
p42 bottom © TFL from the London Transport Collection; p43 ©
Alamy/P.D. Amedzro; p44 © Museum of London Docklands; p45 ©
Science Museum; p51 © Getty Images/Mike Kemp; p54 © Alamy/Simon
Belcher; p63 © ZSL London Zoo; p65 © LEGOLAND Windsor; p74 top
© Alamy/Ken Worpole/Edifice; p74 bottom © Alamy/Pat Tuson; p104 ©
Kidzania; p105 Alamy/nobleIMAGES; p143 © Wellcome Collection; p156
© Tramshed; p157 © Tom's Kitchen; p158, p173 © Kim Lightbody

Design: Sarah Allberrey
Editor: Anna Watson
Commissioning editor: Zena Alkayat

A catalogue record for this book is available from the British Library.

ISBN 978-0-7112-3863-3

Printed and bound in China

9 8 7 6 5 4 3 2 1

Quarto Knows

Quarto is the authority on a wide range of topics.

Quarto educates, entertains and enriches the lives of
our readers – enthusiasts and lovers of hands-on living.

www.QuartoKnows.com

MIX
Paper from
responsible sources
FSC® C101537
www.fsc.org